THE DEADNAME TRIPTYCH

Savannah Manhattan

<u>The Triptych</u>

Dedicated to Dana, Colin, Dayton, Luna, and Arlo for
leading the energy

Thank you to Birdcage Ink for believing in my vision.
You are never alone and there is always a way around fear.

This collection of poetry follows the ethereal bloom of my
transformation from the previous
collection, also available through Birdcage Ink.

While the previous collection focused on a spiritual plane,
this one focuses on me facing the
cityscape in my new mind and body, as well as coming out
publicly and the emotional gamut it
entails. The city is full of opportunity and prosperity, but
also uncertainty and chaos. It is a new
path laid out to sculpt what remains and test who I have
yet to become.

Remember to embrace yourself for who you are because
your vessel has a specific purpose. Solve your puzzle and
carry out your meaning.

Part I

A Paradox of Electrons

A Paradox of Electrons

I'm hunched over

Empty pages

Bathing my room in Bitches' Brew

In a neighborhood with glamour and warfare on both
sides

Stuck in the middle

Stuck in neutral

The blessing and curse of a level pendulum

In medias ras

In perpetuity with no explanation

Only an expectation to know everything already

Not make a single mistake

To avoid pitfalls but not live too easily

Under the thumb of everyone's standards

Overanalyzing

Under-analyzing

Being in radar and out of the radar like the qualia of
fireflies

Under a thumb full of cuticles and strep

It's difficult to elaborate exposition

When you're expected to be everywhere at once

In every time zone

Even pretend ones

Time zones you wish existed just to fit more life into

Give imaginary mass to

We're a paradox of electrons

Here and

There

Simultaneously

So yes

I am hunched in bad posture

Sacrificing vertebrae for chances to be seen and heard

Fighting from invisibility

While immersed in Bitches' Brew

It is important to start there because first impressions are
everything

Just like everything else

The first impression is one thrust into a mold of chaos

A mold requiring its own mold and mitoticly more molds

Amorphic and indefinite

What I learned between my old self and now

That trench of altered states

Within my shimmering, rosegold homunculus

Would shatter anyone

I only have enough pieces of the mirror to show you

Fleeting glimpses

By leading the pace with no choreography
It invites you to trust me as I had to trust my guides out
there

It is terrifying to be curious

Even dangerous, yet it is necessary

Now we must go see this open world before us

This topography of the unknown

Seeing if anything is left for us, or right for us

It is scary but I will no longer bend over my desk in a
blaring room in Los Feliz

It is time to go out, stretch, and put some miles on these
bones

Part II

Deadname Culture

Deadname Culture

A blessing from the Source to cleanse this journey:

Prayers to Dana

Who blesses the Source with beauty and splendor
Render my path without obstacle, only opportunity and
love
Thank you, dear one

∞ ∞ ∞ ∞ ∞ ∞ ∞ ∞

Prayers to Colin

Who blesses the Source with strength and optimism

Help me to see the next step
No matter how dark
Thank you, dear one

∞ ∞ ∞ ∞ ∞ ∞ ∞ ∞

∞∞∞∞∞∞∞∞

Dana and Colin

No evil or primal instinct on my shoulders
Give me weightlessness
Yet keep me grounded between planes
May your gentle hands guide me through
The difficult and the joyous
111 222 333 444 666 000 1111
The code to get in
You both give me will
You give me clarity
You gave me the eye
Blessings to you, Dana and Colin

May we all protect and be protected

∞∞∞∞∞∞∞∞

∞∞∞∞∞∞∞∞∞

Sherman Oaks, 8pm

It begins with a thought
It always has
Logos
The word
The word that sparks the action
Words which carry weight
Camels burdened in a caravan
They say it's the quiet ones you watch for
They are the ones with the most thoughts
The most plans
The most potential energy
Waiting for a catalyst to ignite the kineticism
It is overwhelming to say your truth out loud because once
magma becomes lava
And thoughts become frequency
It also becomes substance
It gains mass
The words drop into the pond
Rippling out with astounding and delicate consequence

I am a woman

A phrase imprisoned in me for years
For crimes it didn't commit
Except being real
I, my own warden

Refusing it release
Knowing if I said it outside myself
It would be final

One day though

Deus ex machina rocketed the vision into me
Hoping I would rocket the truth back out
Centrifugal escape velocity
The scales fell from my eyes
First a contortion
Then a whisper
I I I
Ego based
Condensed down to me and a universe of possibility
Hanging onto the next word
I Am
Forming a tetragrammaton
Granting myself the strained rush of air
Mingling among the muffled TV noise in the living room

I Am A Woman

Booming

Silent

A concussive grenade of admittance
No need for a rosary or a father
Mouth as arid as the Mojave

Eyes wet as Niagra
A landmark all my own
Alone in the room back then
Sitting in shocked finality
Creating myself with the most important string of matter
A logos which made light
The key turned
The prison door opened
A bruised and pummeled essence arose
The first step in a thousand-mile journey
Laid a path
As I tasted the salt of my sadness and disbelief
Enough salt to make Lot's wife
I said it again
Louder
I Am A Woman
More confidently
I Am A Woman
Infused with my new meaning
I AM A WOMAN
Turning static into a clear signal
Walking out freer than yesterday
With a voice that could shake the nation of my identity
Seismic and substantial
Logos ambrosial on my tongue
The hertz surrounded me and electricity was obsequious
They say everything is created twice
The first time when you think it
The second time when you form the clay, fire the kiln, and
let it cool

We were created twice so far
No fine-tooth combed engineering
When we're born
Merely a wish to the wind
Chaotic output

Vulcanized through passion and nerve endings
We grow up as the second version
Fingers crossed
Plunged and plugged in

Hoping for the best amidst the world's needs
The idiom is cracked however
There is a third form
The realization
We are beyond our genetic code
Status quo
Imprisoned behaviors and self-destruction
Planned obsolescence scares us into obsolescence even
faster

Blowing out a flame
Instead of letting the wax melt away
And enjoying the shadows dancing on the wall

There is a third form
A beautiful harmony of polyrhythms
Three over two
Four over three

Ostinatos and syncopation
Playing in a subterranean chasm
80 percent over 20 percent
An iceberg with few daring to swim to the belly
I had no choice but to let go
When the pain became too great
When she kicked and screamed
Battering down my gates on Valentine's Day
Duping every blueprint made for me

The orgasm of my true self
I was reset
All the voice training I ever had
Led me to speak up for once
Shifting from my diaphragm to my nasal cavities
Tightening my throat
Controlling air flow
All to tell the world who I've been this whole time

The tertiary cycle
The substance I kept to myself
Now bootlegged and shipped to whoever needed to hear
The voice built taller than skyscrapers
Scaffolding more reinforced than US Steel
A city all my own
I sat and waited

Knowing I went far from uttering it to the nation of
myself

To a continent of the rest out there

Going from sounding out words like "daughter" and
onomatopoeias
To sharing my penultimate secret
Almost missing being in hiding
Romanticizing having control over something
Yet there is more control
More wealth
More romance
In being undeniable
Not letting anyone else engineer you
Telling them the definition
Showing them the map instead
Putting your foot down all because
You no longer need your feet if you're capable of flight

∞∞∞∞∞∞∞∞∞

∞∞∞∞∞∞∞∞

∞∞∞∞∞∞∞∞

∞∞∞∞∞∞∞∞

∞∞∞∞∞∞∞∞

∞∞∞∞∞∞∞∞

A recipe of who she is

1 head of blonde, roots betrayed
2 hazel eyes
1.5 gallons of blood
200 mg spironolactone
8 mg estradiol
1.4 mg transdermal estradiol
100 mg progesterone
1111 Hz of magnetic field energy

Assemble, mix the pills and elements, and stir with
synapses, chemicals, habits, psychedelics, and
multiple exobytes of memory.

Serving Size: Unlimited number of people if feeling
extroverted

Hypoallergenic, low in cholesterol, low in tolerance of
small talk and stupidity

Feed with care, love, joy, intimacy, parties, road trips,
playlists, massages, money, clothes, accessories,
imaginative cuisine, deep conversation, good books, jokes,
occasional joints, jazz, metal, hair care,
skin care, drums, and especially hot beverages.

Keep in warm areas. Highly flammable. Non-religious.
Non-toxic. Vibrational. Cremate past
expiration date. Look for reincarnation nine days after
that. Don't place around chronically loud
noises or ignorant people.

Preheat with a deep kiss and long hug. Repeat as
necessary.

∞∞∞∞∞∞∞∞∞

∞∞∞∞∞∞∞∞∞

According to "the rules" put in place
Men must have Adam's apples
Chiseled jawlines
A penis and testicles
Confidence and dominance
Means to provide

Women must have soft skin, soft voices
Breasts
A vulva
A uterus
Be submissive and silent

Would you call a man who has a smaller Adam's apple less
of a man then?
Is a woman who went under traumatic hysterectomy or
mastectomy no longer a woman?
Is a man with no jawline feminine now?
Is a woman with confidence masculine?
Where is the line drawn?
It was drawn by shaky hands and careless artists
The "rules" have always been base level and slogged
The game within the game is flawed
We can be anybody
All matters of chemistry and construction
Spectrums with gold everywhere
There is a bridge above us and a bridge below us
What you were given can be kept or passed along

We are not beholden to our default settings
Don't be angry at a machine that upgrades
It works better and you are fossilized and full of virus
Don't be angry if a circle wished to be erased and re-drawn
into a square
Every shape is a gear in the overshape
The Metatron
The exquisite palace
We can be anyone
We can do anything
Temporary is haute couture
Flow state is high fashion
Permanence is cast aside
Far past default setting

The killswitch and its codes are in clandestine bunkers
Laissez faire
Laissez faire
The rules are eradicated
Gorgeous anarchy is the new game
We are the new biology
Play ball
Enter the cube and be kind
We are here

∞ ∞ ∞ ∞ ∞ ∞ ∞

∞∞∞∞∞∞∞∞∞∞

My brother warned me
Before I arrived here
The city is a steamroller

That never stops moving
If you jog ahead
You'll be fine

Stop too long or fall and it will crush you
You can never be idle
The driver has bloodlust on his face
Hungry for a paycheck
No days off

Eager to execute and live up to his quotas
A killer must eat too, right?
Plowing over the unfortunate
The ones who lost their jobs
Missed their own checks
Didn't have a support system
After each life
The devil driver takes a swig from the flask in the glove
compartment
My brother's warning planted a seed in my brain
Next to my bloom
Always find a way forward
Always find a way around
I heeded the soothsayer

Finding solace in the skin of my houndstooth dress
My thigh-high boots
The wingtips accenting my eyes
Giving span to the vision that once was blind
Finding wisdom in the smiles of strangers
Future friends

The clink of plates, glasses, and chatter in restaurants
I used to hide
Believing everyone was staring at me
Fetishizing me
The way their messages appeared on my phone
Was the glassy-eyed gaze they gave me on the train
In department stores
In thrift shops

Equaling the accolades, the compliments, and the saviors
of those who understood me

When I say everything exists
I reminded myself of that over and over
When I was convinced
When I was hated, ostracized
Deemed a monster
I flashed back to the love out there

Fear is a potent minority with the confidence of majority
It all has the same chance of going well as it does going
wrong

Whenever my crude oil casket of a car broke down
Or I was condescended to
Or I lost a job
Or called a man in womens' clothing
Or lusted after and tossed
Or told to be patient for someone else, even if it's my
identity
Or denied work
Or denied healthcare
Or legislated against
Or offered money for porn
Or asked to please respect someone's opinion against my
detriment
Or told I'm not trans enough
Or that I'm trying too hard
Or that I'm selfish for posting photos
Or called by my dead name, now buried
Or told I'm being mourned instead of celebrated
Or catcalled on Rodeo Drive
Or catcalled on Melrose
Or catcalled on Vermont
Or called slurs outside of theaters
Or told I'm against nature
Against biology
Against the law
Judged
Pigeonholed
Obsessed over
Dismissed
Deified

Demonized
Radicalized
Heathenized
Popularized
Canonized
Loved in vain

Whenever I'm cradled in the arms of madness
I see only the face of the steamroller operator
Teeth gritty with viscera
And I remind myself the coin flip has equal odds
When I'm behind in the count
When I'm scrounging loose change from a car seat outside
of Starbucks
When my trailer burns down from arson
When I'm wondering how I'll eat
Where I'll sleep
What I'll wear
Who I am
I flip the coin again
Turn the page
Drink my wine
Focus on streetlights and smokestacks
Knowing the coin will land on heads eventually
In the meantime
I'll just turn heads
While I remain ahead of the homicidal steamroller

∞∞∞∞∞∞∞∞

∞∞∞∞∞∞∞∞∞

The mood swings kicked in today
What I was told was a ghost period

Everything at once
            Out of nowhere
                        Unplanned
                                    Intense
                                            Explosive
Tears from anger

            Tears from how beautiful a song can be

Everything igneous

                        Everything in tundra state

Tandem torment and bliss

                        The pleasured euphoria

A new pendulum
Spontaneous
Merciless
Instead I bleed in other ways
Maybe my blood is an apparition of my memories and
oppressors
My family denying me

∞∞∞∞∞∞∞∞∞

∞∞∞∞∞∞∞∞

Welcome to the game show where she is the subject and
you, the viewers, are participants!
Here are the things you will say about her when you are
around her:

When are you getting the surgery?
So what are you?
He, she, it, I don't know
What are pronouns?
You're so brave, I don't know how you do it
I remember when you were [name redacted]
It's so confusing
Are you a transgender?
What's AFAB?
What's AMAB?
What was your old name?
I identify as an attack helicopter
I don't get it
Trans people in sports
Trans people in locker rooms
What bathroom do you use?
Educate me
Can't you just tell me?
But when ARE you getting the surgery?
You're sinning against God
You're tricking God
T******* are so funny

He/she
What's up, man?
What's up, bro?
The scans of eyes up and down my body
Stop the music!
Round over
How did you do?
No matter how many of those you did
The judges have declared you as having lost the game
No consolation
Parking not validated
You not validated
Please exit the studio

∞∞∞∞∞∞∞∞∞∞

∞ ∞ ∞ ∞ ∞ ∞ ∞ ∞

At an outdoor café for brunch with a friend who says:

You are complete as you are
Even if you don't know it yet
No one else can ever be the last piece
We are within ourselves, whole
Lovers and soulmates
Whatever you label them as

Meant to infuse, augment, add to, compound, layer on
your joy

No one can be your joy except you
Many times, we learn that lesson
We constantly are lonely
Bored with ourselves
Needing someone to fix the ennui like it's a broken fuse
We sleep with people to check off a list sometimes instead
of for the sake of connection

The right people will always be right for you
The wrong will see themselves out, backed by player piano
You are more fine and worthy than you think

∞ ∞ ∞ ∞ ∞ ∞ ∞ ∞

∞∞∞∞∞∞∞∞

Los Feliz, 3pm

Whenever someone struggles
Another struggle triggers
A kneejerk reaction of lethologica
A darkly comforting blanket of words in the short term
Torn away in the long term by housekeeping
Unless you try to understand
You can only capture the outline
The shadow of pain
To face the atom is to be the atom

Until then, anything we say is only a principle of
uncertainty
Most of us know the location, not the speed
Or the speed, not the location
Asymptotic
Infinitesimally close
Platitudes are the toolboxes of cowards
Loosening the bolts that require tightening

Stripping the screw

All we need is the comfort of understanding
Instead of the white noise of pretending we do

∞∞∞∞∞∞∞∞

∞∞∞∞∞∞∞∞∞

Los Feliz, 6 am

Three orange bottles
I shake like maracas
A percussion whose rhythm gets me closer to my highest
self

One bright orange sphere before bed
Giving me curves
Someone would be lucky to coast on

Four blue ellipses
Two in the morning
Two in the evening
Bolstering my estrogen and aligning me
Tasting like sugar

Two beige circles
T-blockers
One in the morning
One in the evening
Coupled with the blue ellipses
Holding back my old chemicals
Bouncers in a dive bar
The masculinity starving in attrition
The tertiary cycle spinning faster

∞∞∞∞∞∞∞∞∞

∞∞∞∞∞∞∞∞

More mood swings in December: a retrospective from this year

Crying to my best friend in North Hollywood
Laughing hysterically in Northridge
Content and well fed in West Hollywood
Dazzled and inspired in Beverly Hills
Frazzled and mired in Sherman Oaks
Isolated and desolate in Universal City
Fashionably freaky in Downtown

Hungry in Little Tokyo
Adventurous in Santa Monica
Overwhelmed by joy in Malibu
Overwhelmed by grief in Van Nuys
Confused in Encino
Cherished in Echo Park
Enthralled in Silver Lake
Mesmerized by Mid City
Underwhelmed in East Hollywood
Gratified in Arcadia
Enamored by the blurs of skylines, these negatives waiting
to be developed

∞∞∞∞∞∞∞∞

∞∞∞∞∞∞∞∞

Beverly Hills, 2pm

It hurts to be told how loved you are
How beautiful you are
How wanted you are
Only to be laughed at and dismissed
When you act out on it

It hurts to be a diamond necklace in a shop window
Lauded and photographed
Yet never sold
It hurts to be raised on a pedestal
Promised divinity by the architects
Only to be passed by and built around by malls and chain
stores

An Ozymandias against your will
Being told you are never alone and when you need them
They shrivel away
The closer you get
The farther they do
Chasing a sunset

It hurts we are born into rules of a plane we didn't choose
To play a game we didn't ask to participate in
With only a puritan tutorial to guide us and no coins for
Chiron

Yes, it hurts
It hurts less though when a bystander finally sees the art in
you
Framing you proudly
It hurts less when you remember you were given your
vessel for you to appreciate
For others to join in that exhibition

You're allowed to worship your own statue if you are one
You are allowed to be loved even when no one else seems
to be
We move through levels because of destruction, not
despite it
When walls crumble and close in, we are meant to run
through

When pressure heats and crushes us
We are meant to be diamonds
When we are stuck in torrential downpour
We are meant to be cleansed
Everything shifts to lead us to the end of the maze

If we are in the game
Then we should play
If it hurts
Then trauma shall be our compost and we will be the
gardeners

∞∞∞∞∞∞∞∞∞

∞∞∞∞∞∞∞∞

∞∞∞∞∞∞∞∞

∞∞∞∞∞∞∞

∞∞∞∞∞∞∞

∞∞∞∞∞∞∞

Downtown, 12pm and Hollywood, 9pm

Already today
I faced office desks
Filling out forms
Feeding the engine of red tape

The hands of notaries and secretaries studying my
evidence
Photos, slips, certificates
Exhuming my old self
Shining fluorescent lamps in some operating theater
Where surgeons vivisected me for the sake of science
The warm smiles of the desk clerks
Reassuring me, devoid of judgement
Happy to help
Refreshing

Stamps gaveled and data processed
In a month's time
I would evolve in the government's eyes
Recognized as someone
Not even my family would recognize
It takes a village to raise a child
Somehow it takes a bureaucracy to raise a trans person
The shovel laid more dirt upon my name
Soon to be another victim of deadname culture

Soon to be a vacant apartment with barely any signs of
former residency
Steps closer to the third creation
When you're out and exposed
You are liberated and naked
No more secrets to carry
Less mysterious
Some mysteries are corrosive
Predisposed to be disposed as nuclear waste
Celebration was in order
Rooftop bars with panoramic view
Patrons with cashmere capes
Furry mules with bumblebees
Hair perfect
Nails immaculate
Worthy of Caravaggio
Lights dancing across the boulevard
Mind hazier with every paloma
A semi-circle of those I love and who love me
Lost in photogenic moments
A Camelot to rival myth itself
Dancing and swaying on the floor together
Mimicking my guides
Delicious Saturnalia
You could serve with mixed greens and mezcal
This was a present celebration for a past moment
However, revelation struck
The future shock bolted me
A flash of where I must finally go
A towering monument

A lone wall below a hill
Stoic and obsidian
Engraved with words
I couldn't make out in my stupor
A vision muddled with near-sightedness
Beckoning me to travel there with the last of my energy

Use the last of your stamina and we will let you sleep
We will keep him at bay
You will see intense pain
Intense tribulation
You will see tragedy below the hill and redemption above
it

Dissolved back out
Friends wondering what I'm deep in thought about
That thousand-yard stare that never left me
The environment otherwise undisturbed
Paying my tab after settling down for a couple more hours
Saying goodbye until next week or so
My mind sharper
The night closing around me as I walk out the lobby
Shrouded around me like my own cashmere cape

∞∞∞∞∞∞∞∞

∞∞∞∞∞∞∞∞∞

City streets, 11pm

The day invites me to wear ornate rings
Large and adorned with citrine
Bracelets with an evil eye centered in turquoise
A necklace with a rhinestone jaguar
Expressing myself as loudly as the jaguar would
The day invites me to cast my shoulders back
Walk with pride
Chin up, eyes forward

Telling everyone I own the space around me

The night creeps in
Scaring away the sun
Intimidating it into warming another part of the world
The night compels me with a deep, cracked voice to
change my jewelry

Long keys between my knuckles
Brightly colored pepper spray
Casting my shoulders forward
Chin down, eyes darting
Telling no one I exist

I've already died and been reconstructed in my image
At my core remains an eclipsed nucleus
My new mantra

Better to be paranoid than dead
Wondering if it's the final walk I'll ever have
I don't feel safe at night
The hue painted on a city
Is the mood it paints on the soul
Graffiti bleeds down the bus stop shelter
Made from prophets of the steamroller:

I am inevitable. I am Legion. I am the one who made
Wilhelm scream. I am the malevolence and
the malediction. I am always next. I am always around the
bend. Face me and you face failure.
You face death.

Having friends used to only mean camaraderie
Indelible experiences
The night tells you friends are a matter of life and death
Function over essence
Friends fill where fathers have failed
We forget humans are animals
Primates by order
Under binomial nomenclature
We forget civilization is a jungle
Where we still need to survive to thrive
To worry when vans slow by you
A dire lesson hormones taught me is to avoid eye contact
Move quickly
Drive immediately
Check my backseat
Don't leave drinks unattended

A lesson a teacher writhes in pain to share

Id is the professor

A lesson half of us are invisible to because they never have
to worry
A problem not happening doesn't mean it doesn't exist
Even if I don't feel safe at night
It doesn't mean I'm not going to wear it like armor
A bulletproof vest
Kevlar against those who wish me dead
I don't feel safe at night

A milestone telling me the pills are doing their job

∞ ∞ ∞ ∞ ∞ ∞ ∞ ∞

∞ ∞ ∞ ∞ ∞ ∞ ∞

City streets, continued, 12am

I'm originally from Minnesota
I drove here some years ago
Wide-eyed and bright
Malleable and culture shocked
The city was another country
This was home all along
The city saw my entire transformation
Hell, it was my transformation
Building me into
MONOLITH
I miss the woods though
The placid lakes
The cries of the loon
The flop of fish
The zip of a tent flap
The deciduous scents
The only woods here are painted on the walls of businesses
Wisps of forest green on a print shop
As I walk down the side streets
I miss the miles of forest
The snaps of twigs
Flutters of indigo bunting
At least I'm home though
Only a couple more miles to go

∞ ∞ ∞ ∞ ∞ ∞ ∞

∞∞∞∞∞∞∞∞∞

Outskirts, 12:45am

I saw it from a distance
Its presence made itself known
Lit by a glow from underneath it
I took a breath to rest momentarily
Studying my surroundings
Suddenly away from the city
I reached the outskirts
An area I have never seen
A mirage of a temporal continuum maybe
Walking closer
I was in awe
The obsidian wall
Looming and waiting
In front of me was a sea of candles
Illuminating the marble
The lights showed me the words that were blurry in my
initial vision
Engraved were the names of my lost people
Filigreed and bold were the names
As bold as their existence when they graced our plane
A memorial wall

Venus Xtravaganza

Svetlana

Pamela Moreno

Carla Leigh Salazar

Rita

Ty Underwood

Sonia Zafra

Agnes Hernandez

Brian Golec

Brandon Teena

Carmen Guerrero

Fernanda Olmos

Amanda Milan

Evan Young

Diana Sacayan

Gwen Araujo

Islan Nettles

Alisha

Nireah Johnson

Dwayne Jones

Hande Kader

Janice Roberts

Jennifer Laude

William Lound

Shelby Tom

Mary Jo Anonuevo

Raina Aliev

Gisberta Salce, Jr.

Kimberly Sody

Paola Ledezma

Latisha King

Cagla Joker

Rae'Lynn Thomas

Angie Zapata

Mahadevi

Jessica Cavalcanti

Lateisha Green

Keeta Bakhsh

Laysa Fortuna

Simmie Williams, Jr.

Sabi Beriani

Amna and Meeno

Victoria White

Aniya Parker

Chanda Sharmeeli

Dee Dee Pearson

Marcela Duque

Bianca

Hilario Lopez Ruiz

Valera

Poe Delwyn Black

Dandara dos Santos

Ebeng Mayor

Ollie Taylor

Wilka

Tyianna Alexander

Tierramarie Lewis

Nataly Briyth Sanchez

Samuel Valentin

EJ Boykin

Alaska Contreras Ponce

Bianca Bankz

Taya Ashton

Jhoana Hernandez

Dominique Jackson

Shai Vanderpump

Kelly Stough

Fifty Bandz

Miss CoCo

Anastasiya Sapaeva

Alexus Braxton

Pooh Johnson

Muhlaysia Booker

Chyna Carrillo

Zoella Martinez

Kiki Fantroy

JJ Bright and Jasmine Canady

Disaya Monaee

Bee Love Slater

Jenna Franks

Brianna Ulmer

Nikki Kuhnhausen

Aidelen Evans

Kier Solomon

Carly VG

Diamond Kyree Sanders

Mel Groves

La Becky

Rayanna Pardo

Royal Poetical Starz

Jesusa Fidel Ventura Reyes

Jaida Peterson

Jessi Hart

Brayan Sanchez Zarate

Dominique Lucious

Jo Acker

Nina Surgutskaya

Remy Fennell

Rikkey Outumuro

Chynal Lindsey

Tiara Banks

Jenny DeLeon

Ozge Bilir

Jahaira DeAlto Balenciaga

Marquisha Lawrence

Patsy Andrea Delgado

Natalia Smut

Alexa Luciano Ruiz

Iris Santos

Serena Angelique Velasquez

Tiffany Thomas

Layla Pelaez

Kevi Washington

Yampi Mendez Arocho

Thomas Hardin

Penelope Diaz Ramirez

Whispering Wind Bear Spirit

Michelle Michellyn Ramos Vargas

Sophie Vasquez

Selena Reyes-Hernandez

Danny Henson

Brayla Stone

Serenity Hollis

To All The Ones Who Took Their Own Lives and To

Those Who Continue to Hide Out of Fear

Behind me I heard a crest of a broken soul
A shorter woman, older
Raven black hair
Face obscured by a handkerchief
Respecting the sea of candles
I watched her solemnly
As she stopped at the wall as I did
Her fingers tracing along the engraved lost
Letting out another wail
She reached into her coat
Pulling out an instrument
A chisel
She stopped momentarily
Frozen in grief

Breaking out of trance, she found a spot under the other
names
As if it waited for her
She cried softly where the pain has the deepest volume
Chiseling into the space on the wall
I stepped closer
Figuring out what she was engraving
A name I didn't recognize
Another woman's name
The woman wiped her eyes and turned
Noticing me for the first time
She said no words but embraced me
Her hug cocooning me
Wishing it was perpetual
She let go and asked if I too lost anyone
I said I have but no one on this wall
She nodded, pointing to the fresh letters carved
Her, my sweet angel Elizabeth
She took her life because I couldn't accept her and I would
give anything to go back and tell her
how extraordinary she is
I would give anything
As she burst into tears again
I held her
A mix of anger
Also a painful understanding
Fury it was too late
Corroded in ignorance
Comprehension it was her hardest lesson to learn
I held her until she pulled away

She planted a kiss on my cheek
She said
You remind me of her actually
You really do
Now I'm going home and do everything in my power to
never turn those in need away
Thank you, dear
The candles illuminated half her face as she turned to look
at the wall once more
Stifling what she could before she left
Exit stage
I waited until she was distant
Walking to where she placed Elizabeth's name
It now shined gold
Another candle manifested itself
Joining the elegy
I felt a mandibular chill
Kneeling down
I kissed Elizabeth's name
Wishing I could meet her
I felt engulfed by the warmth of all
The flames of youth
The overwhelming need to sleep by the wall until daybreak
Where I would ascend the hill and bury my old name
Finally, after all this
I felt safe in the night
I love you, Elizabeth
I love you

∞ ∞ ∞ ∞ ∞ ∞ ∞ ∞

∞∞∞∞∞∞∞∞∞∞

Golgotha, 6:30 am

Have you ever killed a man?
Have you ever felt like Abraham?
Have you ever stood over yourself while it rains
Seeing the horror of power transfer?
You can't be haunted if you don't believe in ghosts
You can't have a chronicle if you don't write the prose
Flows are whitewater rapids
Shifting suddenly
Crashing against jagged mountains
When all you wanted was rest
You first must put yourself to rest
My old self became inertia
I also was my own outside force
Cracking my skull
Sending me running as a pinball
In front of the steamroller
After the tragic wall
I landed at Golgotha
A hilltop haunted by its own ghosts of massive sacrifice
Drawing anyone who needs to let go of what
Doesn't serve them anymore
Seating myself on the soft grass
Bathing in the sunlight that peeked out
Welcoming back my safety after a trying night
Thinking about how my name felt in my mouth
Feeling malignant
Tumorous

Feeling like a used pistachio shell
A kernel in the crevasses of a forgotten wisdom tooth
There is so much quiet here
So much glistening of dew
Staining my pants
No noise of vehicles, espresso machines, or conversation
No Bitches' Brew
Peace and quiet
The hell of the busy man

I was ready to bury my identity so I could show the city
below my new one
With no fear or shame
I was ready to stop being my own human shield
I stood back up and called out to repay
What I was once given
My second creation
No more living life as a negative number
One step forward, three steps back
Time to be a plus, a positive sum
The ones who gave me a name

Danced with me and sent me mercifully back down here
Now required tribute
A gift I could send to the sky
The four letters once a placeholder from my parents
One that served me for years
A name uttered by everyone I grew up with and loved
Everyone who became my angels
I reached into my throat

Right into the pulse
Tearing the old sound out
Thanking it for granting me purpose
For leading me where I am now
I held that name in my hands
Kneading the four letters and rolling them in my fingers
Letting them swim like amoebas of mercury
The name once had power
It was now a dead battery
It became a phantom I needed to exorcise
I called on my guardians
Opening the sky with arms of cumulonimbus
They were ready as well
I let the name float, kissing it goodbye
Floating toward the heavenly dimension
Joining the old vessel I gave
It would now form for someone else
A reactionary energy
Shaping mouths and minds for how to give it to a man
who deserves it
The piece of me that offered me astounding insight
Providing for me
Became dead, buried
Far out of reach

A place where it could only speak through muffled efforts
It was encoded, alien, foreign
Saying it now would either bring forth draconian rage
Or shock, as if you showed me pictures of an autopsy
Only I can carry the key

Once in awhile
I'll creak open the canopic jar and peer in
Entertained by a memory
The birth name is no more
I am the I Am
I am the only one who gets to decide my own name
A respect we should all give each other
I felt the weight lift from my aching shoulders
Pleased for this moment
This slice of time
Where I could just be
The vista of the landscape stretched out in a serene
masterpiece
Painted by the hand of Gaia
My new name from within glowed
Throbbed with heat
Grateful to be granted nascency and genesis
A Sherpa of my mountainous memories and futures
I didn't grieve
I danced
I didn't moan a dirge
I sang a melody of yellows, red, oranges, plums, and robin
eggs
I roared in magnanimous delight
A deep-seated glory radiated outward
I was prismatic
All the colors hidden by a single beam
Now untethered
The nature around me laid quiet
Listening

The wind directed my choreographed whimsy
My joy was a staccato on everything I experienced
A true name
A true body
A true mind
No darkness remained
Ask me what's in a name
I can tell you
Utter purpose
Utter power
Utter reason
Every day
You can thank anything listening for being alive and
connected
Every day you can redefine
Rebuild
Re-siphon
Re-channel
Re-integrate
Transform
You can be anything and everything
You are more than a name
You are a burst of this world
I didn't feel my feet because I ran so fast
Past the memorial wall
Past the silent wildlife
Past the factory buildings, warehouses, street carts,
bustling bars, folks I recognized in a new light
Past every beautiful experience in this city
All the way back home to Los Feliz

I don't remember my head hitting the pillow
I just remember I finally had freedom
Freedom for myself
And freedom from that goddamn steamroller

∞ ∞ ∞ ∞ ∞ ∞ ∞

∞∞∞∞∞∞∞∞∞

A blessing from the Source to purify the end of the road,
laying a path for the new.

To the Source
To angels Dana and Colin
I incant to you my thanks
My gratitude
My humility
You stayed my hand and mind
When my soul and mouth were strayed
You leveled my being
You made the centrifuge a wheel of honor
You made me the fulcrum and the pendulum
The calm inside of the chaos
Bookended blessings you give me graciously
Linear to the untrained mind
Always existing instead
Even in dire times
Throughout all spheres you travel
Throughout all lives you radiate
The seals are opened
Revealing peace not apocalypse
The zero sum
Balance forever
Thank you for rest, for prosperity, and for your glow
Thank you to the Source
Bless you

∞∞∞∞∞∞∞∞∞

Part III

God Duel

God Duel

The greatest joke in the world is thinking you can trick

GOD

A trio of hieroglyphics as sonic singularity

Unscrambling and accordioning out

Into any deity or energy you devise or relate

Vibrations hit our eardrum

Process in Wernicke's area

And cause us to bow, praise, or disavow

Any master or mother who will ease or threaten our

attachment here

The laughter bellows out if you think

Any linguistic interpretation of a cosmic caretaker

Could ever be blindfolded and duped by anything less

than itself

If the deity is infinite

It means it cannot create anything less or greater than

itself

It means we are flawed in every way and no way at all

Everywhere at once

It means we can face it eye to eye

Knowing it can't make mistakes

It is a kneeslapper to think

An infinite being wouldn't know

Our next eight moves and beyond

A grandmaster supercomputer

Calculating who will change and when

The solution to the uncertainty principle

It would know where we're going down to the quark

And it would be pleased

Old models of machines

Tell you you can't trick GOD

Yet that is what we apparently are doing by transitioning

Which means we have more power than infinity

Congratulations

They scream with picket signs and pedagogy

That if you're born that way

You are doomed to stay

Cretaceously encased in amber

The punchline gets a standing ovation every show

If you change against GOD's will

You then killed GOD

Great job

The supercomputer is shut off

Now go back home

Kick off your shoes and watch TV

You really deserve it

After all

With this new responsibility you have

It wouldn't hurt to take a sabbath or two

Savannah Manhattan is the author of *The Deadname Triptych* and *There's Something About Theo*. She lives in Los Angeles.

www.ingramcontent.com/pod-product-compliance
Lightning Source LLC
Chambersburg PA
CBHW020507160726
47991CB00007B/2843